DRASTIC PLASTIC
AND
TROUBLESOME TRASH

WELBECK

THIS IS A WELBECK CHILDREN'S BOOK

**Published in 2021 by Welbeck Children's Books
An imprint of Welbeck Children's Limited, part of
Welbeck Publishing Group
20 Mortimer Street, London W1T 3JW**

ISBN: 978-1-78312-643-9

Printed in Dongguan, China

10 9 8 7 6 5 4 3 2 1

**Executive Editor: Bryony Davies
Design Manager: Emily Clarke
Designer: Darren Jordan
Picture Researcher: Paul Langan
Production: Gary Hayes**

FSC
www.fsc.org
MIX
Paper from
responsible sources
FSC® C144853

**The publishers would like to thank the following sources
for their kind permission to reproduce the pictures in this
book. Key: T=top, B=bottom, L=left, R=right, C=center,
BKG=background**

Alamy Stock Photo: /PhotoAlto sas: 27C

Shutterstock: /Africa Studio: 35L, 40-41BKG, 41TL; /
Aleksandra Suzi: 57BL, 57BR; /AlenKadr: 25TR; /
AlexandrBognat: 57TR; /Alf Manciagli: 44-45; /alfocome:
21TR; /Amberside: 17L; /anek.soowannaphoom: 33BL; /
antb: 60R; /Aphelleon: 4-5BKG; /arikbintang: 55BL; /
Arnon.ap: 24-25BKG; /asliozber: 17R; /azure: 59L; /
Berka7: 32-33BKG; /Bessarab: 18BR, 34C, 42L; /Big Foot
Productions: 4CB, 23BR; /BravissimoS: 58BL; /Chaikom:
5T; /CHAIWATPHOTOS: 4B; /Chaiwuth Wichitdho: 60BL; /
Chocosummer: 43TL; /Christopher Boswell: 26-27BKG; /
Dalibor Danilovic: 8-9BKG; /DAMRONG RATTANAPONG:
42BC; /Dario Lo Presti: 36-37BKG; /Dmitry Rukhlenko:
22-23BKG; /Dmytro Zinkevych: 61R; /donatas1205: 20C;
/Dragan Milovanovic: 15B; /Elena Elisseeva: 55TR; /
Ethan Daniels: 13BR; /Evan Lorne: 56-57BKG, 57R; /
Evannovostro: 47BR; /exopixel: 35C; /FabrikaSimf: 34R,
39R; /foxhound photos: 58TC; /girl-think-position: 26BR;
/gloverk: 25BR; /Guitar photographer: 55BR; /HelloRF
Zcool: 18BL; /Huguette Roe: 10-11BKG; /Jag_cz: 20-
21BKG; /K. D. P.: 42-43BKG; /kamilpetran: 38-39BKG; /
kanusommer: 35TC; /kc look: 9B; /Kenishirotie: 41BR; /
Kira Garmashova: 47R; /Kletr: 28-29BKG; /Kokhanchikov:
31BR; /Koxae Sun: 43L; /Leonid Ikan: 46-47BKG; /
LightField Studios: 50TC; /Luminis: 51TR; /M. Unal
Ozmen: 25BC; /macrowildlife: 37C; /Magdalena Kucova:
27R; /marcin jucha: 58BC; /Mariyana M: 25BL, 26BL; /
Makistock: 18L; /Marius GODOI: 51C; /mbrphoto: 50R; /
Meister Photos: 35TR; /Menna: 35TL; /MidoSemsem:
18TR; /Minoru K: 5CB, 52-53; /MOAimage: 42BL; /
Mohamed Abdulraheem: 6-7BKG; /Mouse family:
34BC; /nelzajamal: 54-55BKG; /Neophuket: 55TL; /
ninefera: 27L; /Oleksandr_Delyk: 49BL; /Olga Gorevan:
60-61BKG; /Olga Vasilyeva: 31C; /onair: 26TL; /phive:
15T; /phomphan: 49TL; /photka: 51L, 59C; /Picsfive:
49BR; /pjhpix: 34-35BKG; /POTILA MR.PHANTONG:
43TR; /pratan ounpitipong: 25TL; /Protasov AN: 26TR; /
Rawpixel.com: 5B, 15R; /Rich Carey: 4CT, 12-13BKG; /
robert_s: 6B; /Rose Seyfried: 50C; /RusGri: 33BR; /
samritk: 33TR; /Sanit Fuangnakhon: 5CT, 18TC; /Sergey
Peterman: 34TC; /Sergey Uryadnikov: 29T; /SHTRAUS
DMYTRO: 39L; /sibadan: 50-51BKG; /Somchai Som: 33TL;
/Sophie McAulay: 59TL; /Subbotina Anna: 30-31BKG; /
SUE WETJEN: 50BC; /Surkov Vladimir: 61L; /Surrphoto:
47TL; /Sutthimon Ounnapiruk: 42BR; /Suzanne Tucker:
11B; /Svetoslav Radkov: 58TL; /T photography: 39BR; /
tamara321: 51TL; /ThamKC: 17BR; /Tommy Lee Walker:
59TC; /traveladdict: 43R; /ugurv: 34L; /vchal: 4T; /
Versta: 18TL; /vipman: 50L; /Willyam Bradberry: 1BKG,
2-3BKG; /Zu Kamilov: 58C

**Every effort has been made to acknowledge correctly
and contact the source and/or copyright holder of each
picture, and Welbeck Children's Limited apologizes
for any unintentional errors or omissions that will be
corrected in future editions of this book.**

DRASTIC PLASTIC

PLASTIC

AND

TROUBLESOME

TRASH

Written by Hannah Wilson

WELBECK

CONTENTS

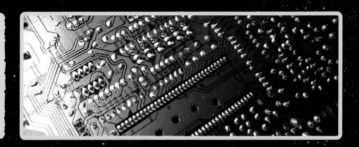

TRASHING THE PLANET

What can you see around you? Plastic toys, an odd sock, a piece of paper? All this stuff is piling up, turning our planet into a trash heap. The way we make, use, and throw away things harms Earth, but we're going to do something about it. Let's investigate plastic, paper, glass, metal, cloth, and food and stop them from trashing the planet.

HUMANS PRODUCE 40 BILLION TONS OF CARBON DIOXIDE EVERY YEAR.

CARBON FOOTPRINTS

A carbon footprint measures the amount of carbon dioxide (and other greenhouse gases) produced by an object or activity. For example, the carbon footprint of a sock includes the carbon dioxide (CO_2) released by growing cotton, making the cloth inside a factory, and transporting the sock to stores.

CO_2 wraps around our planet and, just like a greenhouse, lets the Sun's heat in but not out. As Earth warms, the climate changes. Ice caps melt, which raises sea levels, and droughts, floods, and wildfires destroy the homes of people and animals.

DON'T PANIC!
No one can be perfect. Every now and then, you'll use a plastic bag or forget to recycle. The important thing is to find out what works for you and your family and to do your best. Small steps make a big difference.

IN THE U.S., THE AVERAGE HOME CONTAINS 300,000 THINGS!

REDUCE
REUSE
RECYCLE

REDUCE the amount of stuff you buy. REUSE things again and again (or give them to someone else to reuse). Then RECYCLE to turn your old stuff into something shiny and new.

LOADS OF LANDFILL

Every year, we humans throw billions of tons of trash in the garbage can. It's taken away by trucks, dumped in huge pits, and (usually) buried. This is landfill. Hold your noses—we're going in!

METHANE
As landfill waste decomposes (breaks down), toxic gases such as ammonia are produced, polluting the air. The most harmful gas, created deep within those rotting piles of trash where there is little or no oxygen, is methane. It's not toxic, but it is a greenhouse gas that is 25 times more powerful than carbon dioxide.

BURN OR BURY?
When space is limited, trash is often incinerated (destroyed by burning), rather than put in a landfill. Although the heat produced can be used to make electricity, normal power plants use less energy to do that. Burning landfill trash can also pump out harmful gases, and burning it in this way may make us feel like we don't have to try so hard to recycle.

CHEMICAL SOUP
When rainwater seeps through landfill, it can absorb toxic chemicals such as lead, arsenic, and mercury. The polluted water, called leachate, washes into soil and underground water supplies. Some landfill sites have waterproof linings to stop this. The leachate is collected and cleaned. But the process isn't perfect—the linings can leak, and the cleaning process uses a great deal of energy.

✗ **TIP** ✗

All the plastic toothbrushes you've ever used are probably lying in a landfill. They'll be there for hundreds of years. Try a bamboo toothbrush instead—it will biodegrade (rot away).

THE WORLD'S LARGEST LANDFILLS CAN COVER AN AREA THE SIZE OF HUNDREDS OF FOOTBALL FIELDS AND RECEIVE 10,000 TONS OF TRASH EVERY DAY.

RECYCLING CENTER

Recycling turns old into new and uses less energy than making stuff from scratch. Always squash, crush, and flatten your recycling—if it takes up less space, fewer gas-guzzling trucks are needed to transport it.

SUPER SORTING

We'll soon find out how new things are made from plastic, paper, glass, and metal. But how are those materials separated from each other at recycling centers?

1 Workers pick out plastic bags, clothing, and other items that will be landfilled or recycled separately.

2 An "air knife" blows light paper and cardboard up a huge duct onto another conveyor belt.

4 Magnets extract steel cans, and an "eddy current" creates a magnetic force to push aluminum onto another conveyor belt.

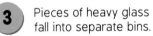

3 Pieces of heavy glass fall into separate bins.

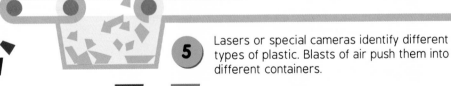

5 Lasers or special cameras identify different types of plastic. Blasts of air push them into different containers.

6 The separated materials are squashed into huge bales, ready to be transported to specialist recycling centers.

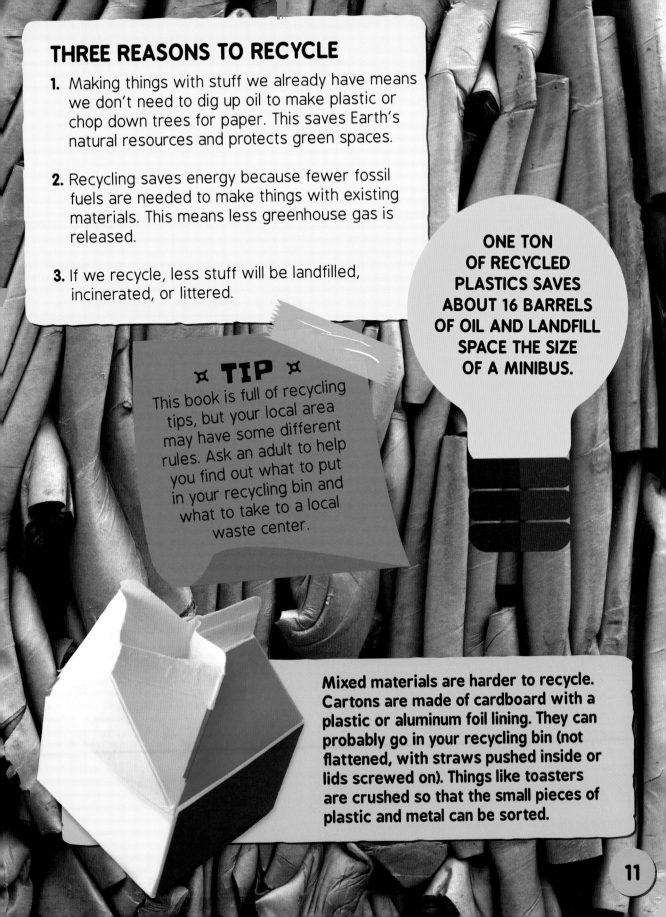

THREE REASONS TO RECYCLE

1. Making things with stuff we already have means we don't need to dig up oil to make plastic or chop down trees for paper. This saves Earth's natural resources and protects green spaces.

2. Recycling saves energy because fewer fossil fuels are needed to make things with existing materials. This means less greenhouse gas is released.

3. If we recycle, less stuff will be landfilled, incinerated, or littered.

ONE TON OF RECYCLED PLASTICS SAVES ABOUT 16 BARRELS OF OIL AND LANDFILL SPACE THE SIZE OF A MINIBUS.

⚑ TIP ⚑

This book is full of recycling tips, but your local area may have some different rules. Ask an adult to help you find out what to put in your recycling bin and what to take to a local waste center.

Mixed materials are harder to recycle. Cartons are made of cardboard with a plastic or aluminum foil lining. They can probably go in your recycling bin (not flattened, with straws pushed inside or lids screwed on). Things like toasters are crushed so that the small pieces of plastic and metal can be sorted.

11

PLASTIC

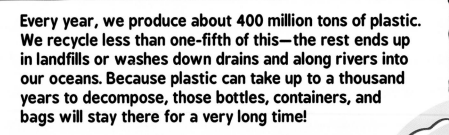

Every year, we produce about 400 million tons of plastic. We recycle less than one-fifth of this—the rest ends up in landfills or washes down drains and along rivers into our oceans. Because plastic can take up to a thousand years to decompose, those bottles, containers, and bags will stay there for a very long time!

EACH YEAR, ABOUT 12 MILLION TONS OF PLASTIC ENDS UP IN THE OCEAN. THAT'S LIKE A GARBAGE TRUCK EMPTYING A FULL LOAD OF PLASTIC EVERY MINUTE.

OCEAN SOS!

To a whale or a turtle, a floating plastic bag looks just like a tasty jellyfish. But the bag will get stuck inside the creature, and poisonous chemicals may leak from it, killing the animal.

Also, over time, plastics in the ocean wear down into tiny pieces less than an inch (a few millimeters) long. These "microplastics" are swallowed by plankton and other small sea creatures. These are eaten by larger creatures such as fish and thus enter the food chain.

Ocean currents wash plastic into huge floating islands of trash. The largest, the Great Pacific Garbage Patch, is twice the size of Texas and contains 1.8 trillion pieces of plastic. In October 2018, a 2,000 ft. long (600 m) U-shaped tube nicknamed "Wilson" was launched, attempting to sweep this plastic up.

MAKING PLASTIC

Plastic is a strong, light material that can be molded into almost any shape, from a hard plastic bowl or thin sheet of plastic wrap to a stretchy pair of socks. If plastic piles up, it pollutes our planet. But the problems begin even before you throw plastic away . . .

PLASTIC FACTORY

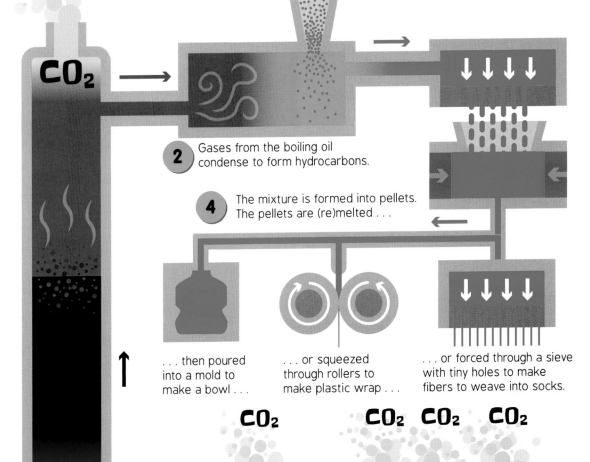

1 Crude oil is heated. Oil contains carbon and releases harmful CO_2 when heated. CO_2 is also released when fuel is burned or electricity is created to heat the oil.

3 Colorful dyes are added, along with chemicals to make the mixture stretchy or flame-resistant.

CO_2

2 Gases from the boiling oil condense to form hydrocarbons.

4 The mixture is formed into pellets. The pellets are (re)melted . . .

. . . then poured into a mold to make a bowl . . .

. . . or squeezed through rollers to make plastic wrap . . .

. . . or forced through a sieve with tiny holes to make fibers to weave into socks.

CO_2   **CO_2**   **CO_2**   **CO_2**

PLASTIC CARS AND PLANES

It's not just toy vehicles that are made of plastic—real-life cars and planes can be up to 50 percent plastic. This makes them light, which means they need less fuel. So, plastic can be energy-saving—we just need to find planet-friendly ways to make it and dispose of it.

Car tires are made mostly of synthetic (human-made) rubber—a type of stretchy plastic. Tiny pieces of plastic rub off on roads and are washed down drains.

TOTALLY TRUE - OR - FOOLISHLY FALSE?

A. Up to 700,000 plastic microfibers are released from polyester or nylon clothes during a single washing cycle.

B. Microplastics are too big to slip through filters in underground drains, so they never wash into our rivers and oceans.

Answers are at the back of the book.

RECYCLING PLASTIC

In the U.S., about 300 million plastic bottles are used every day, and 90 million of these are not recycled! They end up as litter, in landfills, or being destroyed by burning, which produces CO_2.

HOW A PLASTIC BOTTLE IS RECYCLED INTO A . . . PLASTIC BOTTLE!

1 Bottles are sorted into different types, then squashed into bales.

2 Plastic degrades (gets worse) every time it's recycled. It can only be recycled three or four times.

3 Washing removes labels and any leftover liquids.

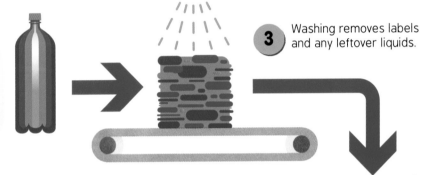

6 The pellets are melted and made into new products, such as carpets, toothbrushes—and bottles!

5 The plastic pieces are heated into a hot, gooey liquid and shaped into strands. When the strands have cooled and hardened, they're sliced into pellets.

4 The bottles are chopped up, and the pieces are separated in a water tank —some plastics will float (including cap pieces), while others won't.

SPOT THE PLASTIC

Look for these symbols on plastic bottles to determine whether they can be recycled.

PET
(Polyethylene terephthalate)
Clear beverage bottles.
Recyclable.

HDPE
(High-density polyethylene)
Bottles for milk and
detergent. Recyclable.

PVC
(Polyvinyl chloride)
Some shampoo bottles,
cooking oil bottles.
Not always recyclable.

PP
(Polypropylene)
Ketchup bottles
and bottle caps.
Not always recyclable.

TIP

For advice on recycling plastics, check your local recycling program, or take a look at berecycled.org.

RECYCLING TIPS

There are many things you can do to help cut down on plastic waste.

 Empty and rinse before recycling. Liquids can damage recycling machinery or other recyclables.

 Crushing your bottles will mean they take up less space, but check your local recycling program for its preference.

 Generally, it's best to keep lids on bottles. They'll be recycled separately.

Make an eco brick by stuffing nonrecyclables into a plastic bottle. This "brick" can be used as a building material. What could you build?

PLASTIC FANTASTIC?

Try to avoid single-use plastics—plastic items you use only once. Can you reuse or upcycle that bottle or tray?

REDUCE AND REUSE

Making a plastic bottle and recycling it both use energy and materials. It's even better to reduce and reuse.

✔ Carry your own water bottle.

✔ Use paper straws or simply sip from the side!

✔ Take your own reusable bags when you go shopping.

✔ Soap up with a solid soap bar.

✔ Donate your old toys to charity.

✔ Bring your own boxes for to-go food.

✔ Try to avoid polyester clothing, or check out special washing-machine bags that collect plastic microfibers.

People power works! In 2016, 385,000 people signed a petition that persuaded the UK government to ban microbeads in toiletries.

DIY UPCYCLING!

Try these cool crafts to transform your plastic bottles and containers. Can you think of anything else to make?

A PIGGY BANK

Cut a slot in the back for coins.

A MODEL AIRPLANE

Use painted toilet paper rolls for jets.

A PEN HOLDER

Glue or tape on a zipper from old clothing.

A SELF-WATERING PLANTER

This plant will take care of itself.

A BIRD FEEDER

Feed wildlife with bottles and wooden spoons.

TIP

Clean plastic bottles, containers, and trays make great bath toys for a small child!

ARE YOU A PROFESSOR OF PLASTICS?

Test your knowledge . . .

1. How long does plastic take to biodegrade?

- **A.** Up to 10 years
- **B.** Up to 100 years
- **C.** Up to 1,000 years

2. Plastic is mostly made from . . .

- **A.** Coal
- **B.** Oil
- **C.** Seaweed

3. Plastic can be recycled . . .

- **A.** 3 to 4 times
- **B.** 30 to 40 times
- **C.** Endlessly

Answers are at the back of the book.

GLASS

Glass is great! We can peer through glass windows and lenses, drink from glass cups and bottles, and use glass to make greenhouses, jam jars, telescopes, and computers. It lasts a very long time, so it must be disposed of properly, but the good news is that glass can be recycled endlessly.

SAFE ON THE SEABED?

Unlike plastic, glass does not release toxic chemicals that smell good to sea creatures. This means it is less likely to be mistaken for food and eaten by a turtle or whale. Heavy and brittle, glass will break into small lumps and sink to the ocean floor, so whales and dolphins can't get stuck in it the way they can in plastic waste.

IT CAN TAKE A MILLION YEARS FOR GLASS TO DECOMPOSE!

SEA GLASS

Tumbling around in the ocean, knocking against rocks and sand, glass breaks into smaller and smaller pieces and is eventually smoothed into pebbles. Look out for colorful "sea glass" next time you're at the beach!

MAKING GLASS

Glass may not cause as much harm to the oceans as plastic, but the way it is produced can still damage our planet. Huge sand mines and energy-guzzling factories create the glasses you drink from every day.

GLASS FACTORY

Glass is made by heating sand and a few other ingredients, including cullet (crushed-up waste glass). The more cullet that is added, the less energy the process of making new glass requires.

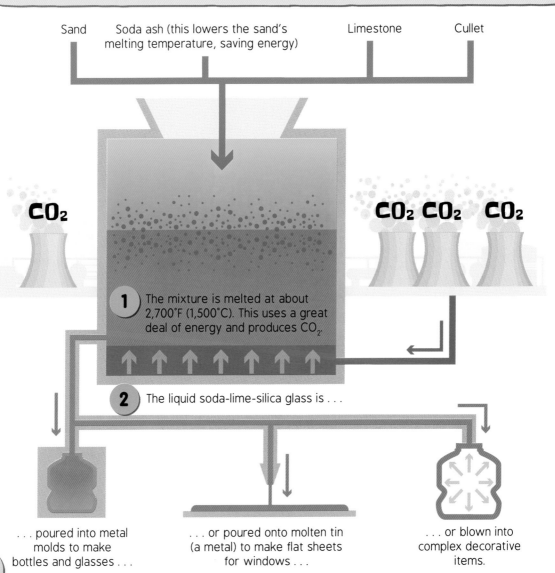

Sand   Soda ash (this lowers the sand's melting temperature, saving energy)   Limestone   Cullet

CO_2

CO_2 CO_2 CO_2

1 The mixture is melted at about 2,700°F (1,500°C). This uses a great deal of energy and produces CO_2.

2 The liquid soda-lime-silica glass is . . .

. . . poured into metal molds to make bottles and glasses . . .

. . . or poured onto molten tin (a metal) to make flat sheets for windows . . .

. . . or blown into complex decorative items.

SAND MINING

The white silica sand used to make glass is scooped up from beaches by huge excavators, or sucked up pipes from river and ocean beds. This sand mining erodes coastlines and destroys wildlife habitats. If more cullet is used in glassmaking, less new sand needs to be mined—so start recycling!

ABOUT 20 BILLION TONS OF SAND IS MINED EVERY YEAR TO MAKE GLASS, CONCRETE, AND OTHER BUILDING MATERIALS.

TOTALLY TRUE - OR - FOOLISHLY FALSE?

A. Some sand is mined illegally—sand thieves once stole an entire beach in a single night!

B. Glass is made with sand and cullet, which is crushed-up waste metal.

Answers are at the back of the book.

RECYCLING GLASS

About two-thirds of glass containers in the U.S. are not recycled. That's thousands of tons of it littering our landscape instead of being turned into cullet! But why is crushed-up glass from our recycling bins and bottle banks so important? Cullet saves CO_2, keeping our planet cool!

HOW GLASS IS RECYCLED INTO . . . CULLET!

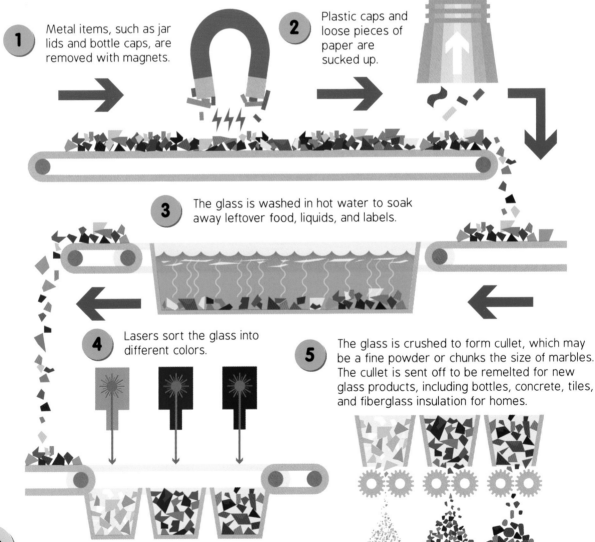

1. Metal items, such as jar lids and bottle caps, are removed with magnets.

2. Plastic caps and loose pieces of paper are sucked up.

3. The glass is washed in hot water to soak away leftover food, liquids, and labels.

4. Lasers sort the glass into different colors.

5. The glass is crushed to form cullet, which may be a fine powder or chunks the size of marbles. The cullet is sent off to be remelted for new glass products, including bottles, concrete, tiles, and fiberglass insulation for homes.

RECYCLING TIPS

You should be able to recycle all glass used for food and drink packaging. For other items, check the labels for symbols that indicate the glass can be recycled:

✓ Rinse glass containers—leftover liquids or food can damage other recyclables, such as paper.

✓ Metal lids are recyclable but often need to be removed. Check your local recycling program to find out what is acceptable.

WHY CAN'T GLASSES BE RECYCLED?

Drinking glasses and heatproof glass oven dishes contain chemicals that cause the glass to melt at different temperatures from jars and glass bottles. They wouldn't mix in properly with the recycled liquid glass, spoiling the process.

EVERY TON OF GLASS THAT IS RECYCLED INTO NEW GLASS PREVENTS ABOUT 600 LB. (272 KG) OF CO_2 BEING RELEASED.

CLASSY GLASS

Before you recycle your glass, try upcycling. Look for jars with unusual shapes or bottles that are bright blue. Whatever you make, place your masterpiece on a sunny windowsill or in front of a lamp and let it light up your life!

REDUCE AND REUSE

Recycling glass is great, but it still uses energy.
Reduce how much you buy and reuse what you have.

✓ Donate old eyeglasses—some opticians collect them.

✓ Give unwanted drinking glasses to charity.

✓ Fill glass bottles with water and keep them in the refrigerator.

✓ Empty jars make great drinking glasses.

One person's trash is another person's treasure! Support recycling by buying recycled products. Look out for drinking glasses made from 100% recycled glass.

DIY UPCYCLING!

Glass is a beautiful material that can throw light around your room. But don't throw glass around the room—it breaks easily, so be careful!

MAKE YOUR OWN JAM

SUPERCOOL STORAGE

A VOTIVE HOLDER

Cut scraps of old cloth to wrap over the lid.

Paint your jars bright colors.

Flames are dangerous —ask an adult to handle the candle!

ARE YOU A GLASS GEEK?
Test your knowledge . . .

1. Glass takes this long to decompose:

A.	10 years
B.	A million years
C.	50,000 years

2. Cullet is . . .

A.	Crushed up waste glass
B.	Sea-worn glass pebbles
C.	A fish related to a mullet

3. Glass can be recycled . . .

A.	1 to 2 times
B.	10 to 20 times
C.	Endlessly

Answers are at the back of the book.

PAPER

We're diving into a digital world, but paper and cardboard still surround us—from the pages of this book to shopping receipts, shoe boxes, and birthday cards. The good news is that paper biodegrades (rots), and it recycles well. For the bad news, we need to take a trip to the forest . . .

WOODCUTTING

Paper is made from wood, so every sheet of paper that you read or write on began life as a tree. It's not always bad to cut down a tree— if it has been planted for timber and a new, fast-growing tree is soon replanted. But it is bad if wild woodlands and lush rain forests are chopped down.

Unlike well-managed timber forests, natural forests are not renewable—they will not grow again quickly. Once an ancient rain forest that is home to thousands of plant and animal species has been destroyed, it cannot be replaced.

TREES ARE TERRIFIC—THEY PRODUCE OXYGEN AND ABSORB HARMFUL CO_2!

MAKING PAPER

Paper is a flattened, dried sheet of mushed-up fibers (strands) of wood. Papermaking is not a perfect process—the factory uses a lot of energy and puffs out harmful gases. Chemicals and inks are added to paper, and these will seep into soil and water if the newspaper or greeting card ends up as litter or in a landfill.

AT THE PAPER MILL

Trees are pulped to make paper. Leftover bark is often used as a fuel to heat the pulp, saving some energy.

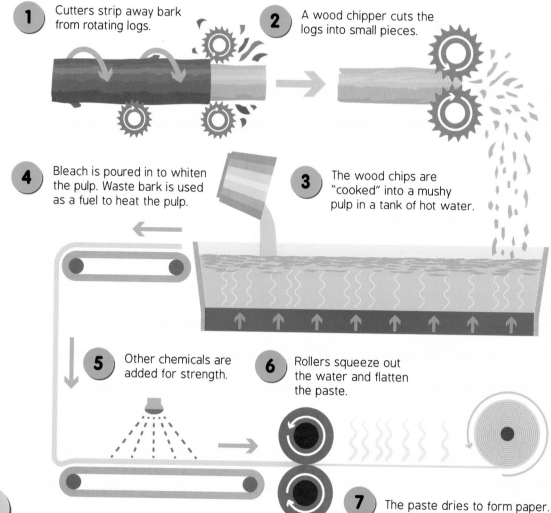

1 Cutters strip away bark from rotating logs.

2 A wood chipper cuts the logs into small pieces.

4 Bleach is poured in to whiten the pulp. Waste bark is used as a fuel to heat the pulp.

3 The wood chips are "cooked" into a mushy pulp in a tank of hot water.

5 Other chemicals are added for strength.

6 Rollers squeeze out the water and flatten the paste.

7 The paste dries to form paper.

PAPER PICNIC?

A paper napkin takes about four weeks to decompose, while paper plates could take five years because they are often coated in a layer of wax, oil, or even plastic. So if you go on a picnic, take reusable plates from home or check out bamboo plates, which are reusable and biodegradable. Perfect!

Bamboo can be pulped to make plates and cups, clothes, and even paper! Whole houses can be built with its strong, woody stems. Bamboo is a good green choice—it can grow up to 3 feet (1 m) in 24 hours (without chemical fertilizers), and it doesn't need replanting.

WHEN PAPER ROTS, IT RELEASES THE GAS METHANE, WHICH IS 25 TIMES MORE POWERFUL THAN CO_2 AT TRAPPING HEAT ON OUR PLANET!

TOTALLY TRUE - OR - FOOLISHLY FALSE?

A. A toxic gas called sulfur dioxide is often released from paper factories, and this causes acid rain.

B. Wood pulp is painted with white paint.

Answers are at the back of the book.

RECYCLING PAPER

Recycling paper saves energy that would have been used to grow and chop down new trees. And it reduces landfill, where paper can take years to decompose.

HOW PAPER IS RECYCLED INTO . . . PAPER!

1 The paper, sorted by color and type, is soaked in a tank of water and chemicals to separate the fibers.

2 The mixture is filtered to remove paper clips, labels, staples, and tape.

4 The pulp (99 percent water, 1 percent fiber) is sprayed onto a fast-moving mesh.

3 A cone-shaped container spins the pulp to clean it. Chemicals may be added to help remove old ink.

5 Rollers press water from the paper, which is then fed through heated rollers for drying and smoothing. Wound onto rolls, the paper is ready to be transported for cutting or printing elsewhere.

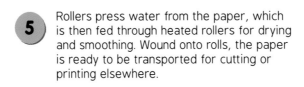
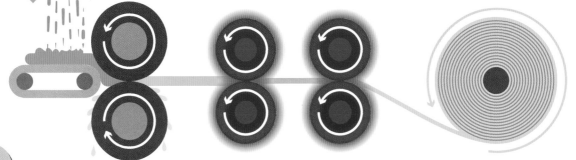

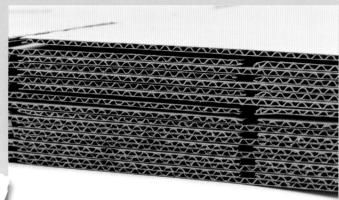

DON'T FLUSH TREES DOWN THE TOILET—LOOK FOR TOILET PAPER MADE FROM RECYCLED PAPER!

Cardboard is brown because it is unbleached (wood pulp is naturally brown). It's often made with pulp from recycled paper. Cardboard must be separated from paper before recycling to stop brown flecks from appearing in the new paper product.

WHAT YOU CAN DO

Find out if you need to separate paper and cardboard in your area.

✓ Do the scrunch test—if the paper remains scrunched, it can be recycled. Nonrecyclable paper (with metal or plastic film on it), springs back into shape.

✓ Remove any pieces of tape.

✓ Greaseproof paper, parchment paper, tissues, wet wipes, and used paper towels can't be recycled—neither can paper with paint on it.

✓ Try to keep paper clean—grease and liquids may mean it can't be recycled.

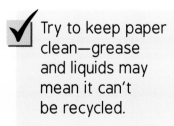

PERFECT PAPER

When you reuse and recycle, you help to save the planet—and you might save some money, too! Why buy something new? Be crafty with old paper around your home.

REDUCE AND REUSE

There are many things you can do to reduce paper usage and make the most of the paper you have.

✓ Use your own cup for to-go drinks. Some places offer a discount when you bring your own.

✓ Try not to print things out—read on screen instead.

✓ Old school notebooks make great notepads and doodle books! Use their covers to make greeting cards or gift tags.

✓ Bring your own box for takeout sandwiches or leftovers.

✓ Donate old books to charity or to your school.

PAPER PRODUCTS CAN ONLY BE RECYCLED ABOUT SEVEN TIMES.

DIY UPCYCLING!

Ask your family if they have old wallpaper, maps, boxes, or books too tatty to be donated. Then start cutting, sticking, coloring, and folding!

! Ask an adult to help you with any cutting.

WRAPPING PAPER

Use pages from magazines or newspapers.

PARTY PAPER CHAIN

Glue or tape paper strips to link loops.

CUP COASTER

A circular coaster image.

Fold up strips of magazine paper and glue them in a coil.

ORIGAMI ANIMAL

Fold up scraps of paper.

PAPIER-MÂCHÉ MODEL

A papier-mâché rhinoceros model.

Mix flour and water to make glue to hold it together.

TRY TO CRAFT WITH SCRAPS THAT CAN'T GO IN YOUR RECYCLING BIN.

ARE YOU A PAPER PRO?

Test your knowledge . . .

1. Which of these can be renewable?

A. Oil

B. Coal

C. Wood

2. Paper pulp is . . .

A. Crushed-up coal

B. Mushed-up wood fibers

C. Mashed-up potato

3. Paper can be recycled . . .

A. 1 to 2 times

B. About 7 times

C. Endlessly

Answers are at the back of the book.

METAL

Have you picked up a steel knife and fork today, pedaled an aluminum bike, or swung open an iron gate? Metal is all around us, but sometimes you won't see it. Precious metals are hidden inside unexpected places.

FOR EVERY MILLION CELL PHONES RECYCLED, WE CAN EXTRACT 75 LB. (34 KG) OF GOLD, 772 LB. (350 KG) OF SILVER AND OVER 17 TONS OF COPPER!

GOLDEN GADGETS

Anything that has a battery or is plugged into a socket uses electricity. Gold conducts electricity (allows it to flow through) better than almost any other material. It can be easily molded into different shapes, and it doesn't rust. Gold is painted onto the green circuit boards that are the brains of computers, phones, televisions, and other electronics.

GOLD MINING

Gold comes from ore—rocks that contain small amounts of metal. The gold ore is drilled or blasted from mines, then the gold is extracted using crushers and chemicals. It's much easier and greener to get gold from e-waste (old electronic and electrical equipment). Up to 800 times more gold can be extracted from one ton of recycled circuit boards than from one ton of gold ore.

MAKING METAL

Metal is a type of mineral, a material that forms naturally in rocks over millions of years. Metals are often strong, shiny, and able to conduct heat or electricity—perfect for making cars, jewelry, cooking pots, and electronics.

STEELWORKS

Steel is the most widely used metal in the world. It's made from iron ore, which is melted inside a superhot, energy-gulping blast furnace.

1 Magnets pull out iron ores from crushed mined rock.

2 Iron ore is poured into a 200 ft. tall (60 m tall) blast furnace.

3 Coke (solid carbon made from coal) is added.

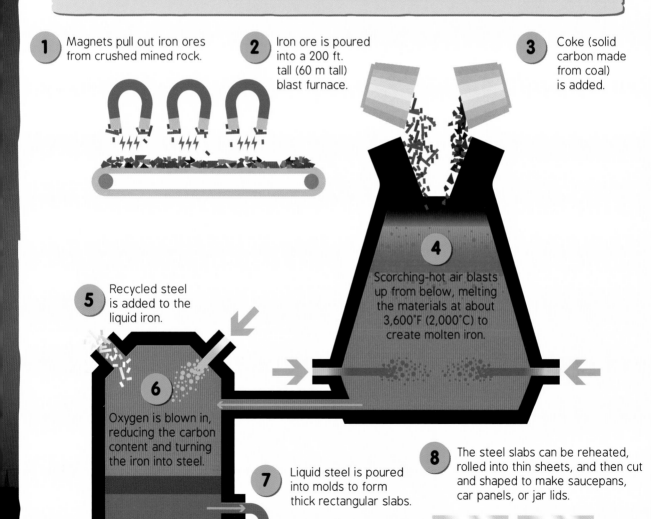

4 Scorching-hot air blasts up from below, melting the materials at about 3,600°F (2,000°C) to create molten iron.

5 Recycled steel is added to the liquid iron.

6 Oxygen is blown in, reducing the carbon content and turning the iron into steel.

7 Liquid steel is poured into molds to form thick rectangular slabs.

8 The steel slabs can be reheated, rolled into thin sheets, and then cut and shaped to make saucepans, car panels, or jar lids.

EVERY YEAR, MINES AND FACTORIES PRODUCE 13 BILLION METRIC TONS OF CO_2. ABOUT ONE-FOURTH OF THIS COMES FROM STEEL- AND IRON-MAKING.

FOSSIL FUELS

Steel-making uses coke made from coal. Coal is also burned inside power plants to make electricity for mines and steelworks. Like oil and gas, coal is a fossil fuel, formed over millions of years from the fossils of animals buried underground. When it is burned, coal releases planet-warming CO_2 and toxic gases.

In many places, the steel-making industry is trying to clean up its act by using less coal and coke. Using scrap steel in the process requires up to 60 percent less energy because there's no need for a blast furnace.

TOTALLY **TRUE** - OR - FOOLISHLY **FALSE?**

A. Blast furnaces are supercool refrigerators that freeze iron.

B. Metals, like fossil fuels, are nonrenewable (not easily replaced or grown again).

Answers are at the back of the book.

RECYCLING METAL

The mining and processing of metals harms our planet, but it's not all bad news. Like glass, metal can be recycled endlessly. Making a can from recycled metal uses a whopping 95 percent less energy than from new metal.

HOW A SODA CAN IS RECYCLED INTO A . . . SODA CAN!

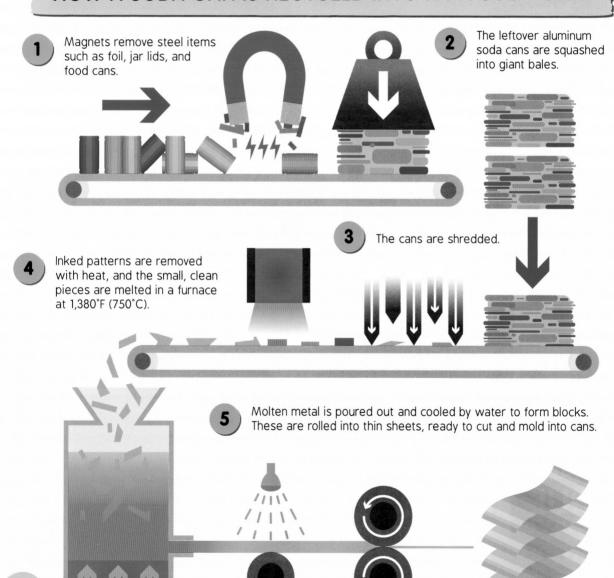

1 Magnets remove steel items such as foil, jar lids, and food cans.

2 The leftover aluminum soda cans are squashed into giant bales.

3 The cans are shredded.

4 Inked patterns are removed with heat, and the small, clean pieces are melted in a furnace at 1,380°F (750°C).

5 Molten metal is poured out and cooled by water to form blocks. These are rolled into thin sheets, ready to cut and mold into cans.

WHAT YOU CAN DO!

There are many things you can do to help cut down on metal waste.

✓ Food cans, drink cans, and aerosols (spray cans) can all go in your recycling bin.

✓ Ask an adult to help you find out where to recycle e-waste.

✓ Dismantle broken toys to extract any metal.

✓ Make a piggybank for small pieces of scrap metal. When it's full, empty it in the metal container at your local dump.

✓ Leave metal lids on glass bottles and jars and recycle them with your glass. They'll be extracted and recycled separately.

✓ Squash together aluminum foil sheets and containers—larger chunks are easier to recycle.

✓ Scrunch-test your foil! If it springs back into shape, it's not foil but plastic with a thin layer of metal. This material, used for potato chip bags, can't go in your recycling bin. It needs specialist recycling.

✓ Batteries must not go in a landfill—they leak toxic metals such as lead and mercury, which poison soil and water. Ask an adult to remove and recycle them separately.

IN 2005, A TWO-TON BRONZE SCULPTURE BY HENRY MOORE WAS STOLEN AND MELTED DOWN FOR SCRAP. THE SCULPTURE WAS WORTH $4.5 MILLION; THE SCRAP ONLY $2,300!

METAL MARVELS

Remember how difficult it is to make steel from rocks? Those metal-rich ores will one day run out. We need to think of all metal as precious, not just the gold and silver that wraps around fingers and dangles from ears. Use (and reuse) it wisely—and have some fun with it!

REDUCE AND REUSE

Making and recycling metal are polluting processes, so reduce your use. Challenge yourself to keep single-use metal (that's foil!) out of the kitchen.

✓ Say no to foil takeout containers —take your own boxes!

✓ If you do use foil, wipe it clean and reuse it.

✓ Rechargeable batteries will help you reduce battery use.

✓ Don't wrap your sandwiches in foil—use a lunch box or a reusable covering.

✓ Donate or sell working e-waste.

✓ Give old cell phones to charity—nonprofit groups often raise money by sending off phones for recycling. Be sure to wipe any data first.

✓ Take an old electric kettle or coffeemaker to a repair shop to be fixed instead of throwing it away.

DIY UPCYCLING!

Make a marvelous metal model! When you've finished
with your masterpiece, dismantle it and recycle.

PLANT POT

Decorate it with little things
you find around your home.

STAPLE SCULPTURE

Stack old, bent staples or paper clips
on an upturned refrigerator magnet.

ETCH A PICTURE

Use the rounded end of a pen lid or
paintbrush to draw on foil!

SILVERWARE CLOCK

Paint the silverware crazy colors!

ARE YOU A MASTER OF METALS?

Test your knowledge . . .

1. Where does metal
come from?

A.	Magnets
B.	Coal
C.	Rocks called ores

2. Which metal do we use
the most?

A.	Steel
B.	Gold
C.	Aluminum

3. Steel-making factories
release . . .

A.	Carbon dioxide
B.	Carbon monoxide
C.	Both these gases

Answers are at the back of the book.

CLOTH

Billowing sheets of cloth in a rainbow of colors are cut up and stitched together to make pants, towels, and curtains. Cloth can be made from plastic fibers or natural fibers such as silk or wool. The most common natural fabric of all is cotton, which begins life in a field.

FIELD TO FABRIC

Cotton is a plant with a hard seedcase that pops open to reveal a ball of soft, white, fluffy fibers. The fibers are harvested and spun into thread to make cloth. Cotton is grown as a crop in warm parts of the world. As our climate changes, these areas suffer from more and more floods and droughts, which devastate the cotton fields.

FARM NOT HARM

Cotton farming often uses polluting chemicals and huge amounts of water, sucking rivers and wells dry and depriving people of essential supplies. But some farmers are learning how to use less water and how to make pesticides from plants. They hope to save money, water, and the planet!

MAKING CLOTH

How many fabrics are you wearing right now? A wool sweater, polyester pants, and maybe underwear with stretchy plastic elastic? You may well be wearing a cotton T-shirt. Let's find out how that's made . . .

COTTON MILL

It takes about 48 hours for raw cotton to be cleaned, combed, and stretched into a thin cotton thread.

1 Raw cotton, harvested by hand or machine from fields, arrives at the mill in huge bales.

2 The cotton is broken apart and blown around to remove any leaves and twigs.

3 Seeds are also separated —they will be used for animal feed.

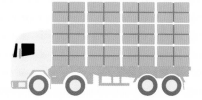

5 A coiler curls out a thick rope of cotton, called sliver.

4 A carding machine combs the cotton with huge toothed rollers. This untangles the fibers and lines them up in rows.

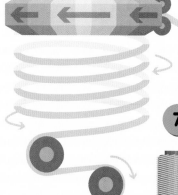

7 The cotton thread is wound onto spools.

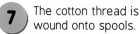

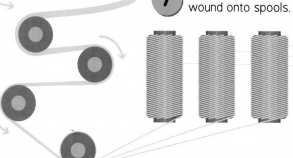

6 The sliver is twisted and stretched over rollers into strong, thin threads.

8 The threads feed into a loom, which weaves them into a sheet of fabric, ready to be cut and sewn into a T-shirt.

CHECK THE LABEL TO SEE WHAT YOUR CLOTHES ARE MADE OF.

ROT OR NOT?

Your cotton T-shirt would take about five months to biodegrade. A wool hat could take one year, and a silk tie could take several years. Your polyester fleece jacket, however, would take hundreds of years to biodegrade!

EVERY YEAR THE CLOTH INDUSTRY USES OVER 100 MILLION TONS OF NONRENEWABLE RESOURCES, INCLUDING OIL, TO FERTILIZE COTTON AND PRODUCE SYNTHETIC (MAN-MADE) FABRICS, SUCH AS POLYESTER.

In the U.S., "paper" money is made with cotton, not paper. Banknotes in Canada and some other countries are made of a plastic polymer film and have the lowest lifetime carbon footprint. They last much longer than paper or cotton ones, so less energy and materials are needed to reprint new bills.

TOTALLY TRUE - OR - FOOLISHLY FALSE?

A. Two-thirds of all the materials used in the cloth industry are made from plastics.

B. A polyester fleece is made from sheep's wool.

Answers are at the back of the book.

47

RECYCLING CLOTH

All cloth, even old rags that your dog has chewed, should be recycled. Natural cotton fibers can be spun into new thread, and polyester clothes can be shredded to make stuffing for couches and car seats.

HOW A T-SHIRT IS RECYCLED INTO . . . A T-SHIRT!

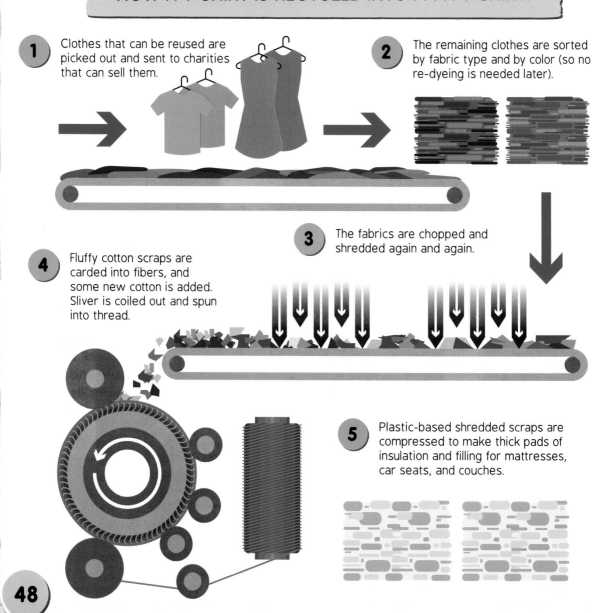

1 Clothes that can be reused are picked out and sent to charities that can sell them.

2 The remaining clothes are sorted by fabric type and by color (so no re-dyeing is needed later).

3 The fabrics are chopped and shredded again and again.

4 Fluffy cotton scraps are carded into fibers, and some new cotton is added. Sliver is coiled out and spun into thread.

5 Plastic-based shredded scraps are compressed to make thick pads of insulation and filling for mattresses, car seats, and couches.

TIP

Use up to 90% less energy by washing clothes in cold water rather than hot. Saving energy also saves money on energy bills!

Shoes can be recycled, too. Rubber sneaker soles can be transformed into springy playground surfaces. Sneakers can also be made from recycled car tires and plastic bottles.

EACH SECOND, ONE GARBAGE TRUCK FULL OF TEXTILES (CLOTH AND CLOTHING) IS DUMPED IN A LANDFILL OR BURNED.

RECYCLING TIPS

Here are some things to remember to help you recycle clothes and other cloth items.

 Fabrics must be washed before recycling.

 Tie pairs of shoes together.

✔ Collect arts and crafts materials—save buttons, zippers, lace, and frills from clothing that can't be reworn.

 To keep them clean and dry, bag your clothes before you toss them in the drop-off bin.

RAGS TO RICHES

Is your wardrobe full of clothes you don't wear? Ignore fast fashion—only buy clothes you need, and wear them until they're too small or they fall apart. Then upcycle your rags into funky new things.

REDUCE AND REUSE

Remember—reducing is always better than reusing and recycling. So try to buy fewer clothes, especially ones made of polyester, nylon, and other plastics.

✔ Donate good-quality clothes to a thrift store.

✔ Repair your clothes —knee patches make your jeans last longer!

✔ Search thrift stores for unusual items.

✔ Use old rags for wiping and dusting.

✔ Host a clothes-swapping party.

✔ Store marbles, board game pieces, and other small items in an old sock.

GLOBALLY, WE COULD SAVE $500 BILLION BY REUSING CLOTHES INSTEAD OF BUYING NEW ONES.

DIY UPCYCLING!

You're growing fast, but you don't need to say goodbye to all your old clothes. Transform them with scissors, sewing, and sequins!

RAG RUG

Tie together twisted strips of rags.

T-SHIRT TRICKS

Frame it or make a cushion cover!

> **!**
> Ask an adult to help you with any sewing— needles are sharp!

SOCK PUPPET

Sew on buttons for eyes and yarn for hair.

RAG BAG

Cut a fringe along the bottom and tie the strips together, then turn inside out.

ARE YOU CLUED IN ON CLOTH?
Test your knowledge . . .

1. Which of these are not made with natural fibers?

A. Cotton T-shirt

B. Silk shirt

C. Polyester pants

2. What do you call the thick rope of cotton coiled out at the mill?

A. Silver

B. Sliver

C. Saliva

3. Which banknote material saves the most carbon?

A. Plastic

B. Cotton

C. Silk

Answers are at the back of the book.

FOOD

Surely a simple sandwich isn't bad for the environment? We all have to eat—food is important and enjoyable—but we need to think about how our food is made, packaged, and transported. Let's investigate the carbon footprint of a ham-and-cheese sandwich.

FOOD FROM THE FARM

A ham-and-cheese sandwich produces 3 lb. (1.35 kg) of CO_2—that's the same as driving a car 11 mi. (18 km)! It takes a lot of energy to farm animals, so the animal products in your sandwich have a higher carbon footprint than the bread or any vegetables you might include. Farm animals also need land to live on, and more land is needed to grow the crops they eat.

IF AN AREA THE SIZE OF A FOOTBALL FIELD WAS FARMED WITH ANIMALS FOR MILK, EGGS, AND MEAT, IT COULD FEED FIVE TO TEN PEOPLE FOR ONE YEAR. THE SAME FIELD COULD GROW ENOUGH FRUIT, VEGETABLES, AND GRAIN CROPS TO FEED UP TO 30 PEOPLE FOR A YEAR.

KEEPING COOL

Sandwiches wrapped in paper and plastic are transported in fuel-guzzling refrigerated trucks. At the grocery store or deli, they sit inside refrigerated cabinets that gobble up electricity. All this adds to the carbon footprint.

A HOME-MADE SANDWICH USES ABOUT HALF THE CARBON OF THE SAME SANDWICH BOUGHT AT A STORE.

As grass digests in their stomachs, cows produce the powerful greenhouse gas methane. Cows burp billions of tons of methane every year, but mixing seaweed into their food could reduce this amount by as much as 99 percent!

MAKING FOOD

When food is processed inside a factory, some weird and not-so-wonderful ingredients may be added. Read the labels on the packaging. Think about how and where your food was grown, the machinery used, and how it was transported.

FOOD FACTORY

To keep food from rotting on the shelf, it's frozen or preservatives are added.

1 Fish is packed into containers and frozen into blocks.

2 The blocks are sliced into strips.

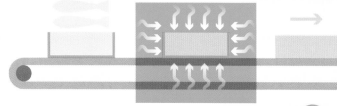

4 The fish sticks are coated in breadcrumbs . . .

3 The strips are dipped in batter made with flour.

5 . . . then flash fried . . .

6 . . . then frozen with a blast of icy liquid nitrogen.

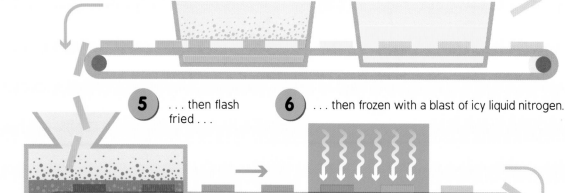

8 The boxes are stacked inside refrigerated trucks and sent off to the grocery store.

7 The fish sticks are dropped into plastic liners, then cardboard boxes.

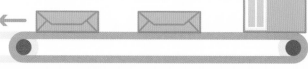

⌗ TIP ⌗

Overfishing can wipe out fish populations, and sometimes dolphins, whales, and turtles are accidentally caught up in the nets. Buy seafood marked "sustainable," which means that wildlife and natural habitats have been treated with care.

WHAT IS ORGANIC FOOD?

Organic food is made without using harmful chemicals to feed animals or spray crops. Chemicals that kill crop-eating insects also kill bees, which fertilize wildflowers and are very important for our natural spaces. The chemicals also sink into soil and wash into rivers, spreading the toxic damage.

THE PALM OIL PROBLEM

When rain forests are cleared to plant palm trees for oil production, animals like orangutans lose their homes. But palm oil can have a low carbon footprint—it needs less than half the land that other crops need to produce the same amount of oil. Look for sustainable palm oil, which doesn't harm natural habitats.

TOTALLY TRUE
- OR -
FOOLISHLY FALSE?

A. Cows burp the greenhouse gas oxygen.

B. You can lower your carbon footprint by eating less meat.

Answers are at the back of the book.

RECYCLING FOOD

Food decomposes easily, so why not just throw leftovers away? The problem is that pesky gas methane—huge amounts are released when food rots in an oxygen-deprived landfill. But recycled food can be made into garden compost, farm fertilizers, and even electricity.

HOW FOOD WASTE IS RECYCLED INTO . . . ELECTRICITY!

1 Food waste is poured into a tightly sealed, oxygen-free tank.

3 As the waste rots, it gives off biogas, which is collected in a huge storage unit.

2 Tiny organisms break down the food in a process called "anaerobic digestion."

4 The waste turns into a sludgy wet mush that can be used as a fertilizer on farms.

5 The gas is piped to homes for cooking and heating water, or to a generator to be converted into electricity.

EVERY YEAR, WE THROW AWAY ABOUT ONE-THIRD OF OUR FOOD— THAT'S 1.3 BILLION METRIC TONS OF ROTTING WASTE, PUMPING OUT 3.3 BILLION METRIC TONS OF GREENHOUSE GASES!

RECYCLING JUST ONE TRUCKLOAD OF FOOD WASTE CAN MAKE ENOUGH ENERGY TO POWER 20,000 TVS FOR ONE HOUR!

COOL COMPOST

Unlike landfills, compost piles contain oxygen, so no methane is created in compost. If you can, compost yard waste and uncooked food waste. Add toilet-paper rolls and cardboard egg cartons for carbon, but not meat or fish. Within 9 to 12 months, you'll have a rich compost for your plants!

RECYCLING TIPS

Find out if your area collects food waste.

✓ Get a small container or trash can with a lid. Line it with newspaper or a biodegradable bag.

✓ Empty all leftover food into the container, even raw or cooked meat.

✓ Make sure there is no packaging mixed in with the food.

✓ Pour liquids down the sink—not into the container.

✓ Keep the container out of sunlight to stop waste from rotting and smelling too quickly.

FOOD FUN

Now that you know about food's carbon footprint and the effort it takes to recycle it, perhaps you'll lick your dinner plate clean! The aim of the game is to scrape as little as possible into your trash or recycling bin. Some food waste (and yard waste) can even be awesomely upcycled!

REDUCE AND REUSE

To reduce waste (and save money), buy only what you need. Think about food packaging—can you reduce that, too?

✓ Overripe bananas can be blended into smoothies or milkshakes.

✓ Sprinkle stale breadcrumbs on soups or home-made fishcakes.

✓ Put fresh leftovers in the refrigerator or freezer, not the trash.

✓ Choose food with less or recyclable packaging.

✓ Reduce your meat—munch on barbecue-flavored crickets for a protein-rich sustainable snack!

✕ **TIP** ✕

Up to 40 percent of vegetables are thrown away because some grocery stores don't like the way they look. Seek out misshapen fruits and veggies—they taste just as good!

DIY UPCYCLING!

What can you whisk away from your food or yard waste to bring back to life?

BIRD FEEDER

Press seeds and leftover fat into a shell or tin.

WORMERY

Compostable waste makes great worm food!

!
Steer clear of old meat and dairy products and anything moldy— they could make you sick.

PEPPER PLANT

Plant pepper seeds in a pot on a sunny windowsill.

GET STICKY

Frame a favorite photo with sticks.

ARE YOU FILLED IN ON FOOD?
Test your knowledge . . .

1. Which food has the lowest carbon footprint?

A. Cheese

B. Ham

C. Carrot

2. Which word describes food farmed without harmful chemicals?

A. Processed

B. Anaerobic

C. Organic

3. How much food do we throw away each year?

A. One-half

B. One-third

C. One-fourth

Answers are at the back of the book.

THE FUTURE IS GREEN

The planet is under threat from our troublesome trash, but scientists are working hard to solve the problem. Some ideas are sensible; others are weird and wacky. But don't forget, YOU now have the knowledge to face the future and paint it green.

NATURE'S INCINERATORS?

Why not blast our trash into the Sun? To launch just one garbage can full of refuse into orbit would cost more than $575,000—and then think of the fuel bill to complete the 93 million mi. (150 million km) trip to the Sun! Or how about throwing trash into volcanoes? They would overflow and belch out horrible trashy fumes, and they're not hot enough to melt metals likes iron and titanium.

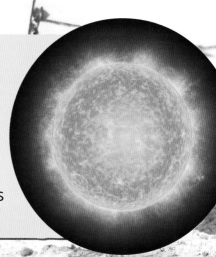

GREAT DEGRADABLES

Reducing packaging is the greenest option of all, but be on the lookout for biodegradable plant-based materials: soaps wrapped in rice paper; plastic-like bags and food boxes made with corn; a mushroom-and-oat recipe to replace the Styrofoam packaging inside boxes. You can even dress top-to-toe in a fabric made from pineapple leaves!

FIVE WAYS TO BE A GREEN SUPERHERO!

Wear an invisible green cape every day and get to work!

✔ Volunteer to be your class recycling monitor.

✔ Go green for gifts —make presents, wrapping paper, and cards from old stuff.

✔ Join a park or beach cleanup.

✔ Write a letter full of green ideas to the government.

✔ Save energy and water—turn off faucets and lights.

✄ **TIP** ✄

Some poorer countries do not have good waste and recycling systems. Check out wasteaid.org. This British nonprofit helps people cope with and earn a living from their trash, collecting biogas from food scraps or building a school with plastic bottles.

GLOSSARY

ACID RAIN
Rain that contains acid formed from factory gases such as sulfur dioxide. Acid rain pollutes Earth's water and soil, kills animals, and wears away metals and stone.

BIODEGRADABLE
Able to rot away into tiny pieces of natural material, helped by natural processes involving bacteria and fungi.

CARBON
A substance that can be found naturally as a diamond or a soft gray-black rock called graphite. Most commonly, carbon mixes with other substances to form new substances, such as the gas carbon dioxide.

CARBON DIOXIDE (CO_2)
A colorless, odorless gas released when fossil fuels such as coal, oil, and gas are burned. Volcanoes produce CO_2, and animals and humans breathe it out.

CARBON FOOTPRINT
The amount of carbon dioxide and other greenhouse gases that an object or activity produces during its whole "lifetime."

CHEMICAL
A substance with a certain group of characteristics. Natural chemicals include gold and salt. Synthetic chemicals are made by people and mixed together to form new substances. Some of these, such as toxic pesticides, can harm the environment.

CLIMATE CHANGE
The changing of weather patterns and the warming of Earth over a long period of time.

DECOMPOSE
To break down into small pieces or rot away.

DEGRADE
To get worse, often in strength, usability, or appearance.

ENERGY
The power from electricity or fossil fuels that provides heat or makes machines move.

ENVIRONMENT
Our natural surroundings, including plants, forests, deserts, oceans, and the air we breathe. Animals, weather, and Earth's climate are also part of the environment.

E-WASTE
Waste from electronic items, which use batteries or electricity. E-waste includes old ovens, televisions, and cell phones.

FERTILIZER
A substance added to soil to help plants grow.

FIBER
A small, thin, threadlike strand.

FOSSIL FUEL
Oil, natural gas, or coal, which formed underground millions of years ago from decomposing plants and animals. Fossil fuels contain a large amount of carbon.

GREENHOUSE GAS
A gas such as carbon dioxide or methane that wraps around our planet, keeping it warm. The gases create the same effect as a greenhouse—they let heat in but not out.

INCINERATE
To destroy something by burning.

LANDFILL
An area or pit where nonrecyclable waste is dumped and stored.

METHANE
A powerful greenhouse gas produced when plant matter decomposes with no oxygen present. Natural gas is mostly methane.

MICROBEADS
Tiny round pieces of plastic sometimes used in shower gel to scrub away dirt. Biodegradable alternatives include ground-up walnut shells.

MICROFIBERS
Tiny plastic fibers that make up plastic-based fabrics such as polyester and nylon.

MICROPLASTIC
Very small (often microscopic) pieces of plastic.

NATURAL RESOURCES
Useful materials, such as wood, coal, and water, that occur naturally on Earth.

ORE
A rock from which metal can be extracted.

ORGANIC
Describing a process that is carried out, or a product that is made, without the use of harmful chemicals. (Organic can also mean "made from living things.")

OXYGEN
A colorless, odorless gas, mainly produced by plants. Animals and plants need oxygen to live.

PESTICIDE
A substance sprayed onto crops to kill weeds, plant diseases, and crop-eating insects.

POLLUTE
To add substances that cause harm, often with chemicals toxic to living things.

POLYESTER
Cloth made from plastic fibers.

RECYCLE
To turn old waste into new objects. The waste is broken up, cleaned, heated, or melted to create new materials.

RENEWABLE
Never runs out, or is easily replaced. Renewable resources include water, air, and carefully managed timber forests. Non-renewable resources include oil, coal, and gas.

REUSABLE
Able to be used again and again.

SINGLE-USE
Used only once before being recycled or thrown away. Packaging is often single-use.

SUSTAINABLE
Describing a process that is carried out, or a product that is made, without long-term harm to plants, animals, or their natural habitats. Sustainability also means that local farmers and factory workers are paid fairly and less pollution is produced.

TOXIC
Poisonous and likely to cause harm to plants or animals.

UPCYCLE
To repair, decorate, or change an object to transform it into something new.